T0120728

A Serious Devotional For the Not-So-Serious

A 30 Day Devotional with Serious Spiritual Thoughts for Those Who Don't Take Life Too Seriously

MIKE NEUMANN

WESTBOW
PRESS®
A DIVISION OF THOMAS NELSON
& ZONDERVAN

Copyright © 2021 Mike Neumann.

All rights reserved. No part of this book may be used or reproduced by any means, graphic, electronic, or mechanical, including photocopying, recording, taping or by any information storage retrieval system without the written permission of the author except in the case of brief quotations embodied in critical articles and reviews.

WestBow Press books may be ordered through booksellers or by contacting:

WestBow Press
A Division of Thomas Nelson & Zondervan
1663 Liberty Drive
Bloomington, IN 47403
www.westbowpress.com
844-714-3454

Because of the dynamic nature of the Internet, any web addresses or links contained in this book may have changed since publication and may no longer be valid. The views expressed in this work are solely those of the author and do not necessarily reflect the views of the publisher, and the publisher hereby disclaims any responsibility for them.

Any people depicted in stock imagery provided by Getty Images are models, and such images are being used for illustrative purposes only. Certain stock imagery © Getty Images.

Scripture taken from the NEW AMERICAN STANDARD BIBLE®, Copyright © 1960, 1962, 1963, 1968, 1971, 1972, 1973, 1975, 1977, 1995 by The Lockman Foundation. Used by permission. www.Lockman.org

ISBN: 978-1-6642-2318-9 (sc)
ISBN: 978-1-6642-2320-2 (hc)
ISBN: 978-1-6642-2319-6 (e)

Library of Congress Control Number: 2021902857

Print information available on the last page.

WestBow Press rev. date: 05/03/2021

To my wife Kathryn.
For your love, devotion, and laughs.
Also your chocolate chip cookies are the best.
Like really. No one is better.

Contents

Introduction ix

Day 1 The Quiet Place 1
Day 2 Spiritual Vagrant 5
Day 3 Fear or Faith 9
Day 4 Your Guide to Being A Super Christian 13
Day 5 A Day in the Life 15
Day 6 Do I Stand or Do I Bow Now 19
Day 7 Divine Combat 23
Day 8 Living on a Prayer Life 27
Day 9 Oh the Things You can Positively Think 29
Day 10 A Tale of Two Brothers 31
Day 11 Good Grief 35
Day 12 Vanity of Vanities 39
Day 13 End Game 41
Day 14 Joyful Joyful 45
Day 15 Get Back Cupid 47
Day 16 Heart of the Issue 51
Day 17 Laying Down the Law 53
Day 18 Shine Bright 57
Day 19 The Man Behind the Curtain 61
Day 20 Justly Merciful 65
Day 21 A Long Time Coming 69
Day 22 Faithfulness of Christ 71
Day 23 My Personal Friend Jesus 75

Day 24   The Chosen One 77
Day 25   Original Sin 81
Day 26   The Reckoning...85
Day 27   The Crowning of the King 89
Day 28   Deep Dish Discoveries 93
Day 29   Hold the Line...97
Day 30   Faithfully Thinking.. 101

Epilogue... 105
About the Author 109
References 111

Introduction

If you're like me, then you grew up going to church. If you're like me (and how could you not be), then you grew up with Christians of all sorts. And if you're like me, certain of those personalities clicked better with you than others. Let me see if this all sounds familiar.

You might be in a typical church if:

- You know people who answer, "How are you" with an emphatic, "I'm blessed!"
- You know people who sing loud and proud, though they are woefully off key.
- You know people who will smile, even if their dog just got run over.
- You know people who are grumpy despite singing about the joy of Christ.
- You know people who use the sermon to "think" of deep things (with their eyes closed because they need to focus).
- You know the person who sprints to the door once the last song is sung like it's the buzzer at a basketball game.
- You know the person who is there because, well, it's the right thing to do.

Does this sound like your church? Here's the secret: that's every church. Every church has a mix of people with their own experiences, personalities, hopes, and wounds. They all influence who we become and how we come before God. Luckily, God has given us a sense of humor. I think that's one of His traits that often gets overlooked. I mean, if He created people, then He must have a sense of humor.

Here's how I imagine this book will work: there will be a Bible passage to read. Start off with a reading so you get the context we are working with. Then there is the meditation regarding the passage. There will be some questions to consider at the end for journaling, to use with groups, or just to make yourself feel super smart. Whatever it may be, make sure to start this process with prayer. Ultimately this is about what God is teaching you and doing in and through you. The book is meant to have a conversational, laid back tone. For some of you who have read other devotionals, this will be a bit different than those.

If you see these people (or even yourself) and can't help but smile and shake your head, then this book is for you. If you're taking life a bit too seriously, then this book is for you (though you may not enjoy it as much). This book gives you some serious thoughts couched in a humorous take. I have found that humor can make truths easier to handle. It diffuses situations that can be hard. My prayer is that this book gives you some thoughts regarding God's word and allows you to enjoy life while interacting with it. May you be blessed in this process. May you be filled with joy.

Day One

The Quiet Place

Read: 1 Kings 19:9-18

My wife's family is a loud family. They are from a suburb an hour west of Chicago, which is part of what's called, "Chicagoland." They are loud, out there, and jovial. My family, on the other hand, are from quiet northern Wisconsin. I remember when our families first met at a place in Wisconsin Dells called Mr. Pancake. My mom and I shrunk away in our seats as her family met us there and exclaimed their joy with the thunder of the heavens. Since then both parties have learned how to "cope" with each other's personalities.

I've always had a quieter personality. For me, I can think better in the quiet moments of life. Don't get me wrong: I love a rip roarin' concert. Nothing gets the blood pumping and gets you feeling alive like a driving bass line and electric guitar. When I need to think though, I prefer solitude. For me, that's when God really does His work. I think that's why this Bible story always meant a lot. Now, some of you reading this may not be the quiet people. Maybe for you, the excitement and drive of life is what's up for you. Perhaps this story helps make the best of those quiet times you have.

Recalling the Bible passage you read today I want you to take a second to look at the story just before this. You see that Elijah is not having a great day. He isn't seeing huge conversions, lives changed, or the church giving out Prophet Appreciation gifts. In fact, in the first eight verses of this chapter, Elijah has a hit out for him by the queen of the land. So Elijah does what any normal, logical thinking person would do: he runs faster than Usain Bolt. That brings us to the story we are at, where we find Elijah hiding by himself and hating life. He is hopeless and feeling like a complete failure. This is when God does His work in a special way.

"How special?" you may ask. Starting in verse 11, we see God demonstrate His power, just like other gods in the surrounding mythologies would have. We see wind, earthquake, and fire. But God is not present in all that power. That's not how He chose to reveal Himself, though He very well could have. That's what makes Him distinctive from the other mythologies. Though God could demonstrate His power with might, He opted for something more intimate. Instead, it is in a quiet whisper that God is heard. In this quiet, intimate moment, God connects with the heart of Elijah and calls him back out into the mission field. He gives Elijah hope of what is to come and gives him a successor, showing Elijah that his labors and struggles will end.

Shh!
God working

When I think about my life, I see God in all moments, but it's in the quietest ones He speaks to my heart and mind in special, unique ways. He has certainly used the exciting and loud moments; the quiet ones, especially when I'm falling apart, is when He does some of His most profound work. I value this story so much because of how faithful God is and the dull, slow moments in life are far from wasted with God. He has purpose and calling for those who call Him Lord.

Some Things to Think About *Brain Stuff*

What describes you best: quiet and reserved or out there and energetic? How does God use that for your calling in life?

How do you find yourself identifying with Elijah? Have there been times when you feel like you got kicked when you were already down?

Thinking on that time, how did you reach out to God? How did He reach out to you?

Consider the quiet moments in life. How is God interacting with you? What is He revealing to you about Himself and why does that matter to you and your calling?

So what? How does this story make sense to the context of your life and how God is interacting with you every day?

Day Two

Spiritual Vagrant

Read: Luke 4:14-21

Now this is a way to start off a ministry, right? In the rest of the story, what Jesus does is basically make people angry because He has the audacity to call Himself the Messiah that was foretold in Isaiah. So how do the people take Him so wildly out of context? What exactly did He say that got them so mad? Well, well, come along with me on this special journey.

Go back and re-read verses 18-19, the ones that Jesus claimed in verse 21 were being fulfilled in their hearing. Jesus is quoting Isaiah 61 and the prophet's promise of the coming Messiah, and what it means. The Jews in the audience remember from their days in Jewish school learning about the prophets that this prophecy concerned the Messiah. What Jesus meant by "this being fulfilled in their hearing" was that He was that guy described in Isaiah. At first the people were confused because He was the son of Joseph the carpenter. How could a blue collar, uneducated wood worker understand the complexities of the prophets?

Here's where things get really good. The way Jesus used these words and the way they were used in Isaiah matched with what He would do later in life. Tim Mackie and Jon Collins (founders of the Bible Project) have a video about the book of Luke. They correctly note that when it says "the poor," it has nothing to do with a financial situation. It is about those who are poor in spirit and hurt. Why is that so controversial? Well, some like to leave well enough alone regarding these people. Why

5

disrupt the status quo? Just toss them a coin and move on with life; I did my good deed for the day. What Jesus was bringing about was a radical transformation to the world and some people got a little bent out of shape. It was more than seeing what someone physically lacks.

Think back to your favorite stories of Jesus. Do you think of beggars, lepers, tax collectors, other "deplorables?" They are all people who are poor in spirit. They are hurt, suffering, and on the business end of injustice. What Jesus promised is what the Old Testament law hinted towards: restoration. The year of Jubilee in the Old Testament was about restoring what was lost and bringing people back to an equal playing field.

In youth ministry my philosophy is highly influenced by this passage. Think about what it would look like if all the students were impacted by this passage and the proper understanding of it. I'm thankful the idea of poor is not money related, otherwise my ministry would have to shell out for iPhones for everyone (unpopular opinion: androids are better). True poverty is about restoration and renewal. That is something teens can understand and, whether they admit it or not, crave. It's what everyone craves. If you're reading this and you follow Jesus, you know how your life has been changed by renewal. Maybe you forgot and need to be reminded of how Jesus changed your life. If you're reading this and you are not on board with this Jesus stuff, I hope this passage is a good starting point to find out who He is and what He is about: bringing people into a relationship with the God of the universe. I promise, you won't be disappointed once you know who Jesus really is, and not like the Jesus the weird perpetually smiley Christian shows you.

Me too! [handwritten marginal note]

Some Things to Think About

Take a minute (or several if you're a slow reader like me) and read all of chapter 4 so you get the context. How is Jesus already bringing this promise to life?

Take a minute to reflect. How are you rich in spirit? How are you poor in spirit? How does Jesus relate to those areas of your life?

What would it look like to be made rich and renewed by Jesus?

Think of someone you know who is struggling in life. What would it look like for them to encounter Jesus? How can you be that ambassador?

So what? How does your story of being made new by Jesus affect others who need to know Jesus?

Day Three

Fear or Faith

Read: Hebrews 13:1-6, Proverbs 1:7, 1 John 4:18

KGB!

As I write this, we are in the middle of the COVID-19 pandemic. You remember that right, where people panicked over something we didn't fully understand? I know that doesn't narrow down things since people do that a lot. In fact, that's the point I'm making. People are naturally fearful creatures. It makes sense. Scientists who study the universe and its origins admit to how the odds of a livable universe are astronomically stacked against us. The universe is in the business of trying to kill us like a KGB agent. A good dose of fear keeps us alive. I'm not saying we should live in fear, but there are times when fear or lack of fear leads people to make, how do I say this delicately, questionable choices. Remember the Crocodile Hunter getting two inches away from deadly animals? On the other end of the spectrum I have a friend from high school who never learned how to drive because he's terrified of hurting or killing someone.

oh my!

I'm not sorry

Let's evaluate the passages we have today. I would apologize for making you read three of them, but it's because you're so special and so loved I just had to put three in there. I promise it all relates though. When we read the Hebrews passage, we see the author pushing for love. Love is the opposite of fear. After all, the 1 John passage tells how perfect love drives away fear. Love is what brings us together and fear is what divides people. Consider the history of humanity when it came to issues of race and culture. Fear of the unknown caused division and atrocities.

I'm a comic book guy. I love reading comic books. My all-time favorite are the X-Men. I love the stories and characters. Fear is a big part of their stories. They are feared for being different and people fear them because they don't understand them. Not only fear of people or attributes about people, but anything unknown. The COVID-19 is an example of how fear is ruling people. For some, it's a fear not routed in the facts. For some, it is a fear that is based on the evidence. For both cases there are sadly plenty of times when people use that fear, healthy or unhealthy, to drive people away or shut them out. For me, I don't fear much, but I hate dark water. I don't know what's down there. I don't think Joe Rogan on Fear Factor could give me enough to hop into open water in the dark! Even in the daylight, I get a little nervous once I can't see what's around me. *Hard pass*

I listened to a podcast by Dennis Prager recently and he made a great point tying Proverbs 1:7 to all this. Someone in a restaurant stopped Dennis and told him how his Bible commentary changed his life. A part the gentleman told him that was most impactful was the idea from Proverbs 1:7. Dennis noted that if we fear God (in the sense of awe and reverence) why do we need to fear anything else? Now this may seem like a, "duh" statement, but how often do we practically use that? How much are our lives ruled by fear?

Two movies give different ideas of how we react to fear. In Frozen, the family reacts to fear in a terrible way. They shame Elsa for what she can't control and hide her away. In the Christopher Nolan Batman films, Bruce leans into the fear and uses it to empower him. Oh yeah, spoiler alert: Bruce Wayne is Batman. I think people, even Christians, follow the Frozen method instead of the Batman method. I will give credit to Frozen that in the end love won out over fear and saved lives. We can be empowered because, if God is for us, who can be against us? When I consider the Hebrews and 1 John passage, I see myself using love to drive me to do what I may be fearful of. If I want my kids to love the water and master it, my fear can't be a driving force. A healthy dose of fear helps us to understand that the water and nature is a force to be respected, but God's love for us empowers us to be in control of how we handle our circumstances. He loves us so much He gave us the will and tools to manipulate the situations. My love for my kids and their passions helps me to fight the fear and my love for them drives me to empower them to live in love, not fear. They have a God who loves them and will care for them.

Something to Think About

What is your greatest fear? How does that impact you?

What causes this fear? Is it a rational fear or is it grounded in speculation?

How does love counter the fear you have? How does the love of God or others move you to action?

How does God's love for you move you to action? What does the way He created you move you to action?

So what? In what ways is God calling you to step out of fear and into His love?

Day Four

Your Guide to Being A Super Christian

Read: Romans 12:1-2

Some of you reading this are *super Christians*. That means you know this passage because you've done the Roman Road study, you've been through Awana and got all the accolades. You are that guy (or girl respectively). You may even have this memorized in Greek or Latin too. Yes, that's the level of dedication you have because (insert trumpet overture) you're a super Christian.

Part of being this super Christian means you know how the world works outside of the Bible's parameters. It means you know that the way people live their lives outside of God's commands leads to lifelessness and lack of meaning. You also know that when it comes to the way of life outside of God's parameters, you're prone to giving into it. Oh yes, even super Christians do that too. Remember that passage before in Romans 3:23? Yeah, that one bites me in the butt too. I shudder to think of how you'd react if you knew my shortcomings in the area of being drawn in by sin. I even shake my head at it too.

Paul writes to the followers of Jesus in Rome. He writes to make a case for how following Jesus is the best way. Through this letter he makes the case for following Jesus and in this section he outlines exactly what we should look like. Paul was very aware of what the Roman way of life looked like. I think that may have inspired his words in chapter one where he talks about people being given over to their desires, especially with issues of sexuality. On the outside it looks like fun, but Paul pulls back the curtain and shows exactly how degrading it really is.

Scary stuff! It doesn't bring about a life of joy or purpose, but instead of loss and sorrow. As I mentioned before, we all fall short, which means we all are prone to the life of the world that goes in opposition of what God has called us to and how He created us to be. Thankfully there's a solution and we find it in Romans 6:23. See how that Roman Road study is coming together?

So how does this all mesh? Point one: we are sinful people and giving into our sinfulness brings about a life lacking in fullness and God's purpose. Point two: although we are dead because of our sins, Jesus brings life to all those who call on Him. Point three: since we are bought back by Jesus, we are to live a life of transformation by God instead of being transformed by the world. We have been created for something greater than the aimlessness of the world's priorities. If you're not a super Christian, this idea helps to kick up your game. If you are a super Christian (though you're humble enough not to admit it), this keeps you being super.

Something to Think About

Reflect to yourself what your big vices or sins are. Which one stands out to you the most? How do you think that vice or sin "helps" you in life?

Take a minute to reflect on the scene at Calvary (see the gospel accounts for details if needed). What does that mean that Jesus paid that price so you can be free of all that sin and vice?

So what? How are you being called to transformation? What specifically does that look like?

Day Five

A Day in the Life

Read: Psalm 23

Yesterday I mentioned the super Christian and how they know about the Bible. Today's passage is one that even people outside of the Church know about. It's popular and is great to slap onto a gift to give it that spiritual lift it needs. I'm sure somewhere out there is a cigarette lighter or a flask with Psalm 23 etched in it. I mean, why not if it sells? I always think of "Saving Private Ryan" with this passage. The sharpshooter on Tom Hank's team would recite this passage before he shot. I'm not saying this makes it for a family night movie; I'm saying it has that kind of cultural gravitas.

Big fancy word!

Whether people recognize it or not, I think what makes Psalm 23 so potent is how it encompasses the human experience. It has the highs, the lows, all framed in the context of how God leads us and cares for us. We can relate to the valleys of the shadow of death. In the Hebrew this term refers to the worst of the worst of times. People in this point in life have despair and hopelessness. Yet we shall not fear because God is our shepherd. When we are exalted and esteemed in front of those who despise us, it's because God raises us up. He provides for our needs physically and mentally. What else could a person possibly want? When we read Psalm 23, it is God who is the center of the story. Re-read it again (I'll wait). It is about what the Lord is doing. This gives a context to the human existence: it revolves around God and His work in the lives of humanity.

I'm not a shepherd nor a farmer, but I know a thing or two about sheep. Did you know that if a sheep falls over, they can't get back up? It's true! I personally get the visual of a sheep on its side with its legs flailing about, much like a turtle on its back. I have a strange sense of humor so this amuses me. Sheep also need a lot of guidance so they don't die, like knowing what pastures to go to so they don't utterly deplete their food source. The analogy of a shepherd so accurately fits with how God cares for us. Ever heard the term "sheeple?" It describes how people can be mindless like sheep and go with the herd. Thinking of yesterday's devotion, you can imagine how people, being like sheep, need a shepherd to guide them where to go and to stay away from harmful situations. Without that shepherd they could be living that life apart from God that brings futility.

I don't think you need to be alive very long to know the human life is a hard one. Sure, if you're born with a silver spoon and a sizeable trust fund, things go a little easier. Even so, numerous studies and personal testimonies demonstrate that money doesn't buy happiness though and the good life is fraught with its own problems. No matter who you are or where you come from, life is tough. What the 23rd Psalm expresses is that longing for someone who is bigger than all this and can be that person you share joy with or that shoulder to cry on. There is something so desperate in the human soul for that person. Jesus gives a face to the God who is that person.

Psalm 23 is a powerful poem. It identifies what people need most and how God meets that need. How blessed we are to have a God who is so intimately involved with His people! Truth is, when we look at other religions and beliefs over time, Christianity and Judaism are the only ones where God is intimately involved with His creation. Christianity takes it further by God becoming one of His creations to live among them as they do, giving His life for them, and rising again to give them a second chance at fellowship with Him. Yeah, I get it. The God of the 23rd Psalm is exactly what I need and want.

Something to Think About

Reread Psalm 23 and let it soak in for a minute. What comes to mind as you read and reflect? What are the mental pictures?

This psalm is attributed to David. Think of what his life looked like. How does this psalm demonstrate a man after God's own heart?

What appreciation do you have for God and His role in your life? How does this psalm reframe that appreciation?

So what? How is God moving in your life to care for you? How does your story tell others of who this God is and why He's so great?

Day Six

Do I Stand or Do I Bow Now

Read: Daniel 3

Still not sorry ←

So this day's passage is a long one. I would apologize, but let's be real: I'm not really that sorry. This is such a well-known story that, if you grew up in the church, you know this. It can be told with anything from puppets to singing vegetables. I wanted to make sure we got the full context of the story because this really is a phenomenal story and incredibly practical for living in a world that is openly hostile to the gospel message. We find that, like our three men in the story, we are often faced with a decision to bow or stand.

The three men are faced with a decision: bow before this idol and save their lives or stand by their convictions to God and face death. It's important to remember these men used to live in Israel. They watched their cities burn and their people either killed or taken into exile. All this happened in their short lifetime. Would you blame them for not having faith in their God? After all, He didn't stop the Babylonians from running their people through. He had stopped it before with other armies (stay tuned for that story another day). Furthermore, in the ancient world, gods were tied to their nations. A victorious nation's deity was assumed to be more powerful than the deity of the nation that was defeated. Yet, while in their lifetime, they watched as God used their friend Daniel to win favor with the king. They watched as they too had won favor with the king.

In the end they took a stand for the God of Israel. They chose to risk their lives for their convictions. As you can guess, the king was

19

not thrilled. Who would've thought a king would be an ego driven megalomaniac? The true heart of the men lies in verses 16-18. Take a second to reread that and make sure it's fresh in your mind. It didn't matter if God delivered them or not. That was not the big issue of the day. They were at peace with the idea that God may not save them and allow for their lives to be taken. It was far more important to honor God than to sell out. Daniel gets the chance to show his metal regarding convictions later too. As we know from the story, they were thrown into the fire for not bowing to the chocolate bunny, uh, I mean statue. We also know how God delivered them and moved in the heart of Nebuchadnezzar.

So what is the point of this story? Is it simply a good children's church story to tell so kids follow what we say? It can serve that purpose, but I think that short sells the story by missing the transformational part. I see this being an example of how these men had an eye to eternity and weren't swayed by the temporary. It wasn't about what God was going to do for them. Don't get me wrong, being spared from this death would be a nice way to go, but they didn't do it to earn a "Get Out of Death Free Card." They did it because they had convictions about who God is and they weren't going to waver. In the end, live or die, their God is over all and they weren't going to compromise that for a statue. God did save them and used this to move in the hearts of many. If you read the rest of Daniel, you will see how God had been working on Nebuchadnezzar.

Something to Think About

How often do you feel like your faith is fighting a losing battle? How often do you feel overwhelmed by what is wrong in the world?

Consider the story of these three men and their faith. Does your faith serve God or you? More specifically, who is the focal point of why you believe: God or yourself?

If you could ask God to reveal Himself in a big way, what would that look like?

Think about how God has shown His faithfulness to you. When was a time He reached out to you when He didn't have to?

So what? When you read this story, how do you see yourself in it? How do you see God using your convictions to reach those around you?

Day Seven

Divine Combat

Read: 2 Kings 19:8-19, 35-37

In the early 2000s, Peter Jackson gave cinematic life to the Lord of the Rings books. They were cinematic gold! Fantastic CGI, compelling acting, and source material that is loved by people of all ages. By far my favorite is the second movie, The Two Towers. Specifically, I love the Battle of Helms Deep. If you haven't seen any of the movies, I'm going to assume you're under 18 and you haven't been able to watch them. I only assume that because if you are old enough, I don't understand why anyone wouldn't want to see them. I'll give a brief overview because I don't want to ruin the epicness. So the heroes are walled in a fortress, trying to withstand the tens of thousands of orcs trying to invade the fortress. Things get really dark and bleak until redemption comes through reinforcements and they survive the night. What a battle!

The passage for today has a very similar picture. Hezekiah is outnumbered and surrounded by the Assyrians. If you remember your world history class, you'd know the Assyrians have a reputation for being cruel and vicious. There is no way Hezekiah can win a battle kinda a big problem through force of arms. To engage the enemy like this is certain suicide. What does a king do? How does he save his people when the enemy has already laid waste to dozens before him? This would be a good place for ominous music...

Look again at verses 8-13. The Assyrians boast of how the Israeli God is weak. It was common to invoke the gods in ancient battles and look to their favor (ever read The Illiad?). The Assyrians sneer at God

23

and say Jerusalem will go the way of the other kings who called on their gods and are dead. Assyria approaches the battle with arrogance and defying God. Hezekiah instead humbles himself and prays to God for deliverance. He showed humility before God and sought His intervention. This was a theological battle being waged and God knew it. He answers Hezekiah's prayer and demonstrates His supremacy over the Assyrians and their gods. At some point, go back and read the part of the story in between our selected passages. That part tells you about what God's response to the king was.

As I mentioned before, a huge component of ancient warfare was about gods battling each other. The winning army was assumed to have the favor of the gods. Sometimes, like in The Illiad (seriously, have you read it?), it is a battle between gods of the same pantheon. As it turns out, battles today really aren't that different. These could be actual battles in war or on social media. Paul picks up this idea in Ephesians 6 with his section on the armor of God. The Ephesians were steeped in black magic until Paul came and shared the gospel. As they turned from their old ways to the ways of Jesus, they were fighting spiritual battles. When we have conflicts, the problems aren't with the person but with ideas, values, beliefs, and sometimes spiritual beings behind the scenes. What I love about this story in 2 Kings is, first, Hezekiah's wisdom to recognize this and humble himself. Secondly, I am impressed by how God flexes on the Assyrians and, when I take the time to humble myself, how God goes before me in my own conflicts. No matter what the conflict is, He is working on me as well as the person I'm in conflict with. Even in The Two Towers, the people who were saved were impacted along with those who were attacking.

Something to Think About

Think about a conflict you've recently had. What was it about? As you dig deeper, what was the core issue?

Was that fight about the person or the ideas at hand?

How did God work on the other person in that conflict? How did He work on you?

Think about other significant conflicts you've had with people. What was the core issue and how was God moving in it all?

So what? How you do approach conflicts? How is God working in you during this time?

Day Eight

Living on a Prayer Life

Read: Hebrews 4:14-16

Smite = bad

At some point, I strongly urge you to read the rest of the chapter. In fact, the rest of the book is worth the time. I'm not saying that the rest of the Bible isn't, but since we are focusing on this passage I wanted to make a plug for the whole book (please don't smite me for the extra work!).

The chapter is about rest and the rest that comes through faith in Jesus. The whole book makes the case that Jesus is the one the Jews were waiting for. As the author writes this part, I am drawn to the idea of prayer. It may seem like a non-connected segue, but stick with me on this. The question I am asking you is, why do we pray? Now you may have numerous reasons. You can pray to ask for something, pray for forgiveness, pray on behalf of another. All of those are great things. There is an undercurrent that connects those. Can you guess it? It's cool to take a minute to think. I'll go get a sandwich and check back in a minute...

So what did you come up with? I know you all are biblical wizards and concluded the undercurrent of our prayers is a connection to something bigger than ourselves. Reread our selected passage again. Then take a minute to read the entire chapter. We can approach Jesus and have His rest because we have a God who is familiar with the human existence based on first-hand knowledge. He didn't read John Piper or Rick Warren to understand people. Not only did He create people, He lived as a person. As a result, we are connecting and talking with a God who knows our ups and downs and has the ability to contend with it all!

What does this look like everyday? Imagine wanting something so bad and praying about it with fervor and earnestness. Imagine what it is like when you get that thing. You're ecstatic! It's so great and you are thankful to God for how He allowed this to happen! The best of times are augmented by our connection to Him because He knows our hearts and saw it fit in the bigger scheme of things to allow us this special treat. Now imagine something terrible happening. It is something that brings you to your knees, literally and metaphorically. Imagine the struggle and the sorrow in your heart because of it. We have a God who understood heart ache and sorrow (see Luke 22:39-46 and John 11:30-37). We can connect with Him knowing He is bigger than all of this and that there is a bigger picture at hand. I can testify that in both the triumph and tragedy of my life, having a connection to something bigger has given it all a fuller meaning. My friends, we serve a great God who can handle all we have! We pray to Him because He can bear all these things and doesn't bat an eye. How wonderful is it to have a God like that in our lives!

Something to Think About

What does your prayer life look like? Does it have a lot of intention or does it slide into empty ritual?

Why do you pray to begin with? What are your expectations of God?

Think about who Jesus is and His experience on earth. What stories of Jesus overlap with you? How do you connect to Jesus because of this?

So what? How does all this help you talk to God and improve the relationship? Does this give you a greater sense of gratitude?

Day Nine

Oh the Things You can Positively Think

Read: Psalm 100:4-5, Psalm 118:1, Colossians 3:15-17

Can you guess what the idea for today is? I'll give you a hint: it starts with "grat," and ends with "itude." Hey, you guessed it! A+ all around! This is a concept that doesn't take much on our behalf but has some big results. As you read the passages and reread them, I want to give special note to Psalm 118:1. That phrase is used in numerous psalms and I'll explain why that is later.

Dennis Prager is the founder of the group Prager University. It's not an actual accredited university, but the title is meant to convey learning. He has a short, 5 minute video about gratitude and it's practicality in life. It's easy to find on Youtube. Gratitude is one of those things that, when present, allow people to be happy not because of what they have or what is happening to them, but because of how they have been blessed. As followers of Jesus, we have that sense of gratitude because of the God we serve and what He has done for us. Remember yesterday's devotion and about being connected to something bigger? That's the idea of why we are grateful.

In the Old Testament, God prescribed holidays and sacrifices with the focus on gratitude. A lot of why He ordained these holidays and sacrifices was so the Hebrews would remember, as it says in Exodus 20:2,

> *"I am the Lord your God, who brought you out of the land of Egypt, out of the house of slavery."*

29

How could you not be grateful to someone who has liberated you and given you freedom? Now I ask this knowing full well what happens to the Israelites and looking at the race riots currently happening today. Both the Israelites then and people pushing for all types of entitlement reforms today have lost that sense of gratitude. Yes, life can be better, that is true. What God was saying to His people then and now is to consider how God has currently blessed you and is continuing to do a good work in you.

Remember how Psalm 118:1 is used multiple times in the psalms? It reaffirms how God is good and His love is constant. God is constantly at work with us because of His great love. He knows what we need and what is necessary for us to grow. Because we are connected to something bigger than us, we can rest in what God is doing in our lives and be grateful for what He has done. It is amazing as I look at the biblical narrative and at the world and see how either gratitude or lack thereof affects people's lives. The disciples gave thanks to God, even as they were hunted, tortured, and killed for their faith because of that connection to Jesus and what He has done and will do. People with very little have gratitude because they are focused on something bigger and better in their lives. I think Dennis Prager is spot on and have seen first-hand how gratitude has changed my life.

Something to Think About

Take a couple minutes and find that video on gratitude. What do you think about it? Do you agree or disagree? Why?

Make a list of the things your thankful for. What is on that list?

As you made that list and reflected, did your demeanor change? If so how?

So what? How can gratitude make your life better? How can you thank God or others for what they have done or their role in your life? How can you continue to live a life of gratitude?

Day Ten

A Tale of Two Brothers

Read: Luke 15:11-32

Ironic...

It really is amazing how Bible stories have such a place in secular culture despite the attempts to rid the Bible from it. This story is one that people who have never read a Bible know about. The phrase, "prodigal son" is known to be about someone who is lost or walked away from their family or group of affiliation. As we read the story, we see the story of a young man who really struggles with taking his father and everything he has for granted. When he asks his father for the inheritance, the son is basically saying, "I wish you were dead." I'm sure many parents have heard their young children say this to them, but it is so much poignant when the child is an adult and fully aware of what they are exactly saying. It really is easy to bag on the younger son since his faults are like shining, bright lights of failure. The older son, on the other hand, struggles with taking for granted what he has.

As we read the story, we see the younger son not being appreciative of what the father has given him. He is missing out on the blessings of the father because he doesn't see what he has. The son thinks he will find greater purpose in the world and when he finally gets the chance, he finds himself woefully mistaken. That's because he's trying to find purpose and identity apart from the father (sound familiar?). He returns with his tail between his legs and finds grace. The older son, on the other hand, knows where his place is. He stays faithful to his father. At the end of the story, when the younger son returns, the older son throws

31

a fit because, in his words in Luke 15:29-30 (according to the NASB translation),

> *"Look! For so many years I have been serving you and I have never*
> *neglected a command of yours; and yet you have never given me a*
> *young goat so that I might celebrate with my friends;*
> *but when this son of yours came, who has*
> *devoured your wealth with prostitutes, you killed the*
> *fattened calf for him."*

This, "son of yours" huh? Quite the shade he's throwing. The father responds by saying that all the father has is the son's. It always has been. It wasn't contingent on his behavior. He took for granted what the father has and never used or enjoyed what was rightfully his. The older son put his identity and purpose in his work, not who he was in relation to his father (sound familiar?). Now, I'm not a family therapist, but I'm guessing this family will need a session or two, maybe seven, of therapy.

Even today we find people who could fit into each category. There are some that have a relationship with Jesus but don't fully realize or utilize what God has given them or what their faith opens up to them. There are others who want their, "Get Out of Eternal Punishment Free Card" and leave the rest. Both people are not understanding what the gift of Jesus is about. Yes, it opens us up to eternity with God. In Christian terms, we call that heaven (or paradise for you educated smarty pants that are familiar with classical literature like <u>The Divine Comedy</u>). It also brings heaven on earth. It allows for God's will to be here and now, not just a future anticipation. It gives us the fullest of life because we are utilizing the gifts God has given us to the fullest. In the story the father, a metaphor for God, reaches out to his sons offering them full access to what he has. Why? Because of his great love. Yes, God's great love has more for us than we really understand. How do we access this? Continue to pursue that relationship with Him through study of His word, fellowship with those who also believe, talking to God, and the continuous process of listening to His leading. You have been created for so much more than we really understand. Your purpose and identity are routed in God and who He has created you to be. In this you will find the fullness of life and paradise (there you go smarty pants).

Something to Think About

Do you identify as the older son or the younger son? Why?

How do you think God has gifted you? How are you using those gifts?

Now consider your relationship with God. On a scale of 1-10 (1 being low and 10 being high), how would you rate your closeness to Him?

What do you do or can you do to help cultivate that relationship? How does this help you understand or better use your gifts?

So what? How are you want to see yourself transformed as you grow your relationship with Him?

Day Eleven

Good Grief

Read: 1 Thessalonians 4:13-18, Psalm 34:18, Revelation 21:1-7

It was early January of 2020. Christian rap artist Toby Mac got the news that every parent dreads. His twenty-one year old son was dead. A few days later he pens the song "21 Years," telling of his process of the grief he is going through as he lives on without his son. It is a commonly held sentiment that the worst thing that can happen to someone is to bury their child. As a father of three little ones, I hope this is a hardship I never have to endure. I can say with full transparency that this is one of those things that may very well break me. Toby Mac is a man of faith. He incorporated his faith into the grief. Yet, as rightfully noted by a college classmate, the church doesn't really talk about grief all that much and if they do it's indirectly.

I chose the passages I did for today because it is important to remember the end game. For those who follow Jesus, to lose sight of that is to lose hope. Eternity gives purpose to the way we live now. If not for eternity, today's actions have no meaning. Yet from day one God created us with an eye towards eternity. It is one of the reasons Jesus went to the cross and rose again. Without that, it would make sense for us to be stuck in the here and now. Let me be perfectly clear: grief must happen and for everyone it will look different. Please don't understand this as a, "pull yourself up by your bootstraps" kind of thing. In fact, we read about how various characters in the Bible, Jesus included, dealt with loss and had to grieve. In 2 Samuel we see how David dealt with the loss of his son and before that the loss of his friend Jonathan. Jesus, in John 11, knew He was going to raise Lazarus but was still moved to tears by the sorrow of the people around Him. Jesus knew He was going to be raised back to life after the cross but still felt overwhelming grief in the garden the night before. He felt the sorrow of His own impending death. That end game is important to keep in mind as we move through the process.

If you listen to Toby Mac's song, his concluding stanza says,

> *"21 years makes a man full grown/*
> *21 years what a beautiful loan/*
> *21 years I loved every one/*
> *Thank you Lord for my beautiful son."*

His eye was on eternity and the end game that comes with our faith in Jesus. Without that, what do we have to rejoice over? The end of pain comes, but they transition into nothingness if Jesus was never raised from the dead. In 1 Corinthians 15:12-19, Paul makes that case that if Jesus was not raised, then we are the most pathetic, sad creatures of all. That's because our hope is a joke and we're the punchline. Now, if Jesus was raised from the dead, then we are beacons of hope for something wonderful, something profound.

Obviously, I don't know most of you from Adam. What I can assume is that if you're reading this, you're a human being, which means you were created in God's image. That means you have the ability to think, feel, and access the spiritual. Being that you're human, it is a high likelihood you will experience grief and loss of some sort. Whether you are currently in the grieving process or some day will be, may you find hope in what God is doing now and will do in the future. Hold on to what He is doing. Re-read the Revelation passage. That is the great hope we have. That is the great hope we can share with others. Soon, very soon, we will be made new again.

Something to Think About

Think about a loss you have experienced or one that you will some day face. What do you remember feeling or thinking? If you are thinking ahead to the future, what do you think you'll be feeling or thinking based on who you are?

How much does your relationship with Jesus influence your reaction? What context does it give to your grief?

Think about what is promised for those who call Jesus Lord. What are you most excited for? How does this influence how you process grief?

Why is it important to have the proper understanding of what God is doing?

So what? How can our stories of grief be beacons of hope for others? How can we share this hope with others outside of the faith?

Day Twelve

Vanity of Vanities

Read: Ecclesiastes 1:12-15, 12:9-14

Oh yes, today is a real "upper." If Ecclesiastes could be summed up, it's this: everything is pointless. How would you like to hear a high school or college graduation address quoting this? Nothing motivates hard work and integrity like saying it's a pointless endeavor. Well, let's hold that thought. I promise holding that thought is not meaningless. I know someone out there thought they were being so smart by saying, "Why should I if everything is meaningless?" I see you...

The first passage tells about what the book of Ecclesiastes is about. For the context of today's devotion, I strongly encourage you to read through the entire book at some point. The Preacher, as the speaker is known by, tries to find purpose from anything and everything under heaven. That means he tries to find purpose in anything except God. The book catalogs his quest. In the end, he concludes with the idea he first put out: Vanity of vanities. That means everything is meaningless. He found fleeting pleasure in his quest. Sure, it was all good for a while as he indulged in knowledge, food, wine, women, and so on. At some point, he felt empty. There is a psychological term called the law of diminished return. This says that as a person indulges in something, they constantly need more and more of that thing to feel the same levels of pleasure because their brain becomes accustomed to the stimulus. For example, if a person uses alcohol to get a buzz, at a certain point they will need more and more to get the same feeling. That's what the Preacher is feeling here.

His conclusion is summed up in the last passage and it tells what the meaning of life is. Nothing on this earth gave him lasting pleasure or anything that fulfilled him. Once he turned his focus to God and His prescription to life, there was meaning. Even these things he chased after, with a godly perspective, had purpose and meaning. For example, food brought joy then because it was based on the prescriptions of the Creator.

Living in a chaotic world can make anyone feel like life is meaningless. With all the chaos and turmoil in the world, it's hard not think about how life is terrible so why not indulge and get what you want out of life. What Jesus offered while on earth was something greater than what this earth has. That's why He told his disciples that He was going to prepare a place for them. That's why the disciples gladly put their lives on the line for the faith. They knew what was on this earth was fleeting and there was something so much greater for them. Tim Mackie and Jon Collins of the Bible Project point out that we are only exiles on this earth and our real home is not here. But that idea I'm saving for another day.

Something to Think About

What is your go-to feel good thing? What do you enjoy about it?

Is this feel good thing used to medicate when you're having a bad day or struggling in life? What does it do for you?

Think about the law of diminished return. How do you see your feel good thing acting like that?

How can you start putting focus on God instead of on your feel good thing? How can having that thing in it's proper place make it more enjoyable?

So what? What can you do to help keep things in their place and God in the place He should be? Who can come along side you and help you with this?

Day Thirteen

End Game

Read: Jeremiah 29:1-7

"I remember it fondly, back in 586 BC. Yes, the Babylonians were razing the city and we were taken into captivity. They were the best of times," said no one ever at that time. The Holy City had fallen and God's people were taken into captivity. A small percentage were left behind but most were deported to Babylon to live out their days there. The prophet Jeremiah was blessed enough to be there and see this happen. I had to use the word "blessed" because in church nothing is bad. We are always blessed. In fact, Jeremiah predicted this was going to happen. The promise of Abraham looked broken. What do they do in this foreign land with foreign gods? The prophet delivers God's instructions for them during this time.

What God asks of them may seem counterintuitive. It would almost seem like they are being asked to cave to the Babylonians. Tim Mackie and Jon Collins of The Bible Project have a video covering this idea. It's called "The Way of the Exile" and it describes precisely this part of the story. God was disciplining His people for their chasing after other gods and child sacrifices. Even so, discipline comes to an end at a certain point and if you read further in the passage, God promises to bring them back to the land. They are called to continue on with their lives and thrive because that is pleasing to God. At the same time, they are to keep in mind that this is not their home and they are exiles in this land. Their home is out there and some day they will return. There

41

were a few prophets God used during the Exile period to remind them of God's faithfulness and His restoration of His people.

Flash forward to Christianity. Tim and Jon correctly point out this exile theme for Christians in the world we live in. Remember yesterday's exposition of life being meaningless? That's because we weren't meant to be permanently in this world. We were always meant for fellowship with God in paradise. Well, it was that way until these two people messed that up *cough cough Adam and Eve*. We are exiles in this land. Our home is out there and some day we will be home for good. In the meantime, make a life and prosper. That is pleasing to God to see His people thriving. It also tells others about the God who loves them and is not bound by circumstances that are unfavorable. Daniel and his friends are prime examples of how their thriving in exile told others of who God is. Same thing is true for Esther and how God used her favor in the king's eyes to save the Jews. At the same time, as Tim and Jon point out, we are to call out evil and be ready to defend what is good and true. We know what is good and true because God is good and true. The way of the exile isn't about keeping your head down and waiting for heaven. It means defending what is right but with humility and gentleness. Read Daniel and watch how he approaches the king. He does so with humility and gentleness, but never strays from saying what is true.

Yeah, I get it, that the world seems to be going downhill at an exponential pace. There's bloodshed, corruption, infringement of human rights, and the list goes on. It will not be this way forever. I read the end of the Bible and (spoiler alert!) God wins. This evil will not endure forever. Justice will ultimately be found and it still can be found now. Continue to thrive. Continue to have families, to laugh, love, and be merry. Continue to fight for what is just and uphold God's standards so others can come to know Jesus. Just like the Preacher in Ecclesiastes, keep your eyes on eternity. There is where we will ultimately live. Until then, God has some pretty great plans for you while you're at this detour.

Something to Think About

In what ways does it seem hard to make it in this life? How does it seem like an exercise in futility?

In what ways has God blessed you so you do well? Revisit your list from the gratitude day if it helps.

How do those blessings tell others who God is and what He has done in your life?

What do you anticipate most when we finally get to our final, eternal home?

So what? How do we live the way of the exile?

Day Fourteen

Joyful Joyful

Read: Galatians 5:16-24, James 1:2-4

[handwritten margin note: I need my safe place!]

Today we have a little different perspective than the meaningless stuff. Ecclesiastes was about how meaningless everything was apart from God. *[handwritten frowning face drawing]* Today, we focus on the opposite of futility (or at least one opposite): joy. Some of you may be thinking joy is synonymous with happiness. Well, I'm going to burst your happy bubble then. Joy and happiness are not the same, though they can be accompanying each other. I have found through study of the Bible and throughout my life that God is not really concerned with my happiness.

Now stick with me. If you still need a comfort blankie, go ahead and grab it and then we'll get into what we mean by that. Happiness is wonderful and God delights in our happiness. Matthew 7 gives that notion when Jesus talks about God delighting in giving what we ask. Here's the tricky part of happiness: it's circumstantial. That makes sense since happiness is an emotion. When was the last time you saw someone happy at a funeral? If you did, that may be reason for suspicion. May want to check on that cause of death again…

Joy on the other hand is one you may find at a funeral. That's because joy is a state of being and a stance of the heart. Joy has to do with a perspective or attitude. I included the passage from James to show how joy is not circumstantial. James advocates we are joyful in hardships because James' is advocating a perspective that focuses on the larger picture. James is connected to someone bigger and a purpose bigger than what's around him. As tradition holds, James died in a horrible way because of his faith. This connection to something bigger makes circumstances like death a minor inconvenience.

The Galatians passage was selected to show how against human nature this is. Joy is something divine. The human nature is to gripe, complain, fall into the, "Woe is me!" mentality. That's what happens when the focus is happiness, not joy. This is evident with entitlement mentalities in every generation. Our circumstances, which much of the time is beyond our control, dictate our mentality and subsequent actions. Joy, on the other hand, looks to the Creator and the Good Shepherd (Psalm 23 anyone?) for how we live. This is a powerful statement to those outside of the faith about who our God is and what He is doing in our lives. Read 1 Peter 3:15-16 to see how this joy can be a witness for others.

These are the reasons why God is not so concerned with our happiness. Happiness is wonderful and God takes delight in our happiness, but it does little for us in the long term. God is interested in winning our hearts by causing true transformation. He is also interested in calling the lost because of the true transformation. Joy is a part of that transformation. So have joy: God cares about your well-being. He just has a bigger, fuller idea of what that looks like.

Something to Think About

What is the difference between happiness and joy? What does each one look like?

How does one begin to cultivate joy?

How do you see a heart of joy affecting your life?

So what: what does joy in your life tell others? Think of someone who could benefit from seeing your life filled with joy because of God.

Day Fifteen

Get Back Cupid

Read: 1 John 4:7-14

Love is one of those nebulous things. It's hard to pin down exactly what it means but we know it when we see it. I think that's because love can be manifest in various ways. Today we aren't focusing on romantic love. So that means no hearts, chocolate candies, or overweight, naked babies with proficient archery skills at shooting people in the butt. This type of love has to do with the way we interact with anybody and everybody we meet, even those we don't like.

It is not uncommon for Christians to complain how the English language is bothersome because it uses one word, love, to describe a multitude of meanings. As I've learned to study the Bible more, I have found this idea to be uninformed. Sure, English uses one word to describe a variety of meanings, but when it comes to the Bible the meaning of the word is in the context. Who would've thought that context would inform an idea. Novel, isn't it?

The passage in 1 John describes where we get love from. We get it from God and it is because what He has done for us. It wasn't because of romantic ambitions that God did this. If He was part of the Greek pantheon then it might be up for consideration. God did this because of how people were created in His image and precious to Him. We get that idea from the first three chapters of Genesis. What that means for people who call Jesus Lord is that we exemplify this selfless love to others.

One word used in Greek for love is *phileo*. This word is where we get

Philadelphia from, referring to brotherly love. This is the idea we see in this passage. You don't need to know a person personally to treat them well. We see people as being created in God's image. We see them as having a value that can only be quantified by the death and resurrection of God's own son. This is why Jesus tells His followers to love their enemies and pray for those who persecute them. It is contrary to what people want to do. It is a sign to those outside of the faith about who our God is. Romans 5:8 says,

> "But God demonstrates His own love towards us,
> in that while we were yet sinners,
> Christ died for us."

Then in verse 10 it reads,

> "For if while we were enemies we were
> reconciled to God through the
> death of His Son, much more,
> having been reconciled, we shall
> be saved by His life."

At some point we were God's enemies. God is completely justified to wipe us from the face of the earth because we violated His law and He is justified to destroy us. We messed up His natural order of the world. Yet, instead of that, we are given a chance. God sends His Son to take the punishment for us to have a fighting chance. That is love. That is why we turn the other cheek. That is why we pray for those who do us wrong. That is why God is the example of love. By following His example, many more can have a relationship with Jesus.

Something to Think About

What was a time you experienced a great act of love? What happened?

Think about how love (treating people well because they are made in God's image) can affect people you see in your life everyday.

How is loving your enemies so different from the way the world does things? What does that claim make about the way of life we have?

So what? How can you affect the people around you (friend or foe) with acts of love?

Day Sixteen

Heart of the Issue

Read: Matthew 9:9-13, Mark 2:14-17

I'm amused that this story is recorded twice and how it is written. I use the NASB version and in mine the two stories are almost word-for-word identical. There is one notable exception: Matthew included a final comment to the story. Now if Matthew was written by Matthew (who was Levi the tax collector), I'm not surprised he included this detail. It's a big deal!

I included both passages in today's devotion because of the context around the story. Both passages are in the middle of stories about Jesus questioning how the rituals in Jewish culture are being carried out. Jesus isn't saying they're pointless; He was a Torah-observing Jew. For those of you new to the Bible and Christianity, the Torah is the first five books of the Old Testament which had the Jewish law that all Jews followed. In there were regulations for sacrifices, fasting, prayer, and so on. We will explore that idea in the coming days. So when Jesus was confronting these issues, He's not trying to knock the idea. God gave these rituals and methods to the Jews. What Jesus is confronting, as He did in Matthew 6, is the way the rituals are done and the heart issue behind them. Jesus really was concerned about our hearts. What a guy!

All this relates to how Levi was treated. He was a pariah to society because he worked for Rome and, much like his fellow tax collectors, pocketed a little extra for himself. Jesus is calling for a reform to the way the Jews did life. Yes, they were called to be set apart and to get sin out of their ranks. What the Jews missed in all this is that they were a beacon of light to the others. They were to call their own people back and restore them to fellowship with God. Jesus' purpose was to bring restoration to all. If words and ways got in the way of that, then something had to change. People take priority over ritual.

What does this have to do with anything today? Last I checked, as Christians, we aren't doing Sabbath (though it's not a bad idea), fasting, or ostracizing others, despite how tempting it might be to do so. When we as Christians do things like fast, rest, baptize, do communion, or any other practice, it is to love God and love others. In Mark 12 Jesus sums up all the Old Testament laws into two: love God and love others. When we are doing these practices, we need to keep in mind our purpose is to share Jesus with others. That may mean evaluating every so often to make sure we are still on target. An example from my life was when I prayed. Before meal prayers became empty rituals so I adjusted it and instead pray before bed with my kids and wife. It may mean changing the way we do things so we line up with the Bible and help others find Jesus. Let me be clear: we follow these practices as the Bible describes, not the way people do. God had rituals for His people in the Old Testament so they would remember what He had done for them and share that with others. The focus was on communing with God and reaching people for Him, whether Jew or Gentile. Knowing how God is concerned about people finding their way back to Him, I am confident we can make tweeks that line up with the Bible and reach others.

Something to Think About

What Christian practices/rituals do you do? How do they help you with your relationship with God?

How do these practices tell others about your relationship with God?

What changes with these practices do you think would help your relationship with God and with others finding Jesus?

So what? How are these practices being used for God's glory?

Day Seventeen

Laying Down the Law

Read: Exodus 20:1-17

If you grew up in the church like me, you grew up seeing The Ten Commandments hanging on the wall of the church somewhere. Maybe it was a Sunday school room or maybe it was in the bathroom stall. I guess for some that spend a lot of time there it will help with memorization. The point is these are incredibly well known in Christianity. What is sometimes missed I think is how the first one really sets the stage for how God is calling His people to act. The immediate context tells us He is talking to Israel, but we can see how well this translates over to Christianity.

First you have to understand what brought Israel to this place. I'm sure you remember the story of Moses, the plagues, and all that jazz. The Israelites have crossed the Red Sea and are at the foot of Mount Sinai. God gives them what they will call The Law. This governs how Jews will live even today. When God did all this, He had to start from scratch with Israel in a sense. Part of what the pharaoh did (which was genius) was to take away the people's history. They lost who they were and where they had come from. That was a big part of why the boys were killed. It left them void of purpose and without a history to fall back on. Not only was it genius; it was sinister. When the Israelites are liberated and arrive at Sinai, they are having to learn a new culture and be reminded of who they are.

That brings us to our passage at hand. What would be the pivotal foundation needed for establishing a people, especially a people that are going to be around other peoples who don't follow God? God starts the orientation with the most essential of truths: He is the Lord their God who brought them out of Egypt and they shall have no other gods before Him. Look at the how the other commandments are contingent on this fact being foundational. Why bother resting if you don't have a God to connect with? Why bother respecting human life if we are not made in God's image and He is sovereign over all? The way we conduct our lives is because we have a relationship with the God of the universe and He establishes the rules and order of life.

Frank Turek is an apologist with Cross Examined. He co-wrote the book <u>I Don't Have Enough Faith to be An Atheist</u> and wrote <u>Stealing From God.</u> The last book makes the case that all morality comes back to God and in order for anyone to have a moral standard apart from God they basically need to rip off God's ideas. Racism is wrong because God created people in His image and calls us to honor all life. Without a God who has that standard why bother? Wouldn't it be advantageous to crush others to make sure we aren't crushed? Why bother being faithful to a spouse if there isn't a God who set the standard? Wouldn't it be better to have fun with whomever, whenever? All this comes down to God calling us to a higher standard that opens to a life full of promise. After all, the guy who set the bounds of the world and how everything works probably knows a thing or two how life works.

God calls His people to a higher standard. He knows where they came from and where they are going. He knows the people groups that will be around them and He knows these Israelites are going to bring about His gift to the world: His Son. The Israelites are beacons of hope for something bigger, something greater than this world and even greater than these commandments. That is why He establishes this first ordinance and calls them to something profound: holiness. We will get into that tomorrow…

Something to Think About

Why does this first command matter so much? How does it set the tone for the rest of the commandments?

Think about the biblical story of Israel. What happened when they kept this command? What happened when they neglected it?

Read Mark 12:28-31. How does Jesus view the greatest commandment? Why does that matter in regards to how Christianity looks?

So what? How does this commandment help us demonstrate who God is and what He is doing for people?

Day Eighteen

Shine Bright

Read: 1 Peter 1:13-16

My brother and I grew up in north central Wisconsin. It is populated by people of mostly Germanic, Scandinavian, and Polish backgrounds. There were Native American reservations in the area too. My brother and I are adopted from India. Other than the Native Americans, who stayed to themselves mostly, my brother and I were the only non-Caucasians in the area. Being the only non-Caucasian people made a couple of things really easy for us. First, playing Kick the Can at night was easy. When you blend in the dark naturally, those games are ones where we can dominate (and we did). Second, it didn't take much for us to stand out.

When my brother was in high school, he played basketball. To go with his white or blue uniform, he bought yellow shoes. Not only was he the only Indian person on the court, he had these bright yellow shoes to boot. He wore them proudly as he moved back and forth on the court. He really was easy to spot. I tell you all this because that's what holiness is like. The definition of holy is to be set apart. When we read in the Bible that God is holy, it is saying He is set apart and there is no one like Him. In Christianity we believe God is on a level on His own. Satan may be His antagonist, but Satan isn't His opposite. To say that is to say Satan is just as powerful and such, but in the other direction. Sorry little red dude, but you can't get on His level. Since God is holy, He calls His people to be so too.

The first chapter of 1 Peter is about how the people are changed by their salvation in Jesus. In the passage you read today, you see Peter use the phrase, "You shall be holy, for I am holy." He is quoting from Leviticus 11. In the middle of giving these laws on what is clean and unclean, God tells His people Israel to be holy for He is holy. He does it again in 19:2 as He begins to talk to His people about forbidding idolatry and then again in 20:7 in regard to human sacrifice. Why does God repeat this? In Leviticus, God is setting His people up to live in a land with other peoples. Their land will be surrounded by other people groups too. The call to be set apart is to distinguish themselves from the other peoples. That's why God has some strange dietary laws, laws that condemned idol worship and graven images of Him, and laws that forbid human sacrifices. These were all practices of the peoples around Israelites and God wants His people to be different because they have a hope and are a symbol of who God is. The practices of the people groups in the Promise Land had to do with worship to their idols. God called His people to a higher standard and to worship Him in a holistic way.

Flash forward to Peter in the first century. Peter is echoing this refrain because Jesus called His people to be set apart. He called them to pray for their enemies. He called them to go the extra mile when asked to do one. He called them to be humble and meek instead of domineering and aggressive. All of this was meant to show who their God is and what He is doing in their lives. That is one part of it at least, a part that brings others to know who God is.

There's one more part about the holiness thing. In the Old Testament, it allowed Israel to be pure so they could be in God's presence. When Jesus died and rose again, He made it so we can be made pure because of His sacrifice. That's part of the idea of the Holy Spirit indwelling in us. We are made holy so we can be in God's presence and we are given a cause to tell others about our God. Holiness matters because it allows us to be with our Creator and to draw others to Him. No yellow shoes required.

Something to Think About

How do you think the Old Testament Law helped the Israelites be set apart?

How could that have helped the other nations know who the God of Israel was?

Think about your walk with Jesus. How are you pursuing holiness? How does that strengthen your walk with Jesus? How does that help your testimony to others?

So what? How is your holiness impacting those around you who follow Jesus and those who don't?

Day Nineteen

The Man Behind the Curtain

Read: Isaiah 6:1-7

You guys have been doing such a good job thinking about holiness, I thought why not one more. What's that you say? You feel so blessed to be on this journey and treasure the extra day to contemplate holiness? I have guided you into exponentially deeper spiritual levels? Well thanks guys. You're all too kind.

Today's passage is a fascinating story. Here we have the prophet Isaiah face to face with God. He sees this great vision of His throne. There are angels, a smoke show, and loud proclamations. It's a marvelous sight that Isaiah is privileged to see. What does he do with such an awesome display? He does the only thing that he can in the presence of this sight: he realizes he is done and he cannot be in the presence of such majesty.

We talked about holiness and the idea of being set apart. We talked about how holiness holds us to another standard because we are focused on a holy God and His attribute of holiness influences us. When Isaiah gets to stand in the presence of a holy God, all He can do is see how unholy and sinful he is. God then does something special. He sends one of the angels down to purify Isaiah, imparting His holiness to Isaiah. What that means is that Isaiah is made clean and can stand in God's presence.

In the Old Testament, we read in the Law about rituals to be pure. Tim Mackie and Jon Collins explain this in their theme video "Holiness" with The Bible Project. It talks about how these rituals made

Israel pure so they could be in God's presence. Without it, they would die. We see this with Isaiah, but instead of symbols for the people to be made pure, God cleanses Isaiah outright. This then launches Isaiah into his ministry as a prophet.

Good question

Being in God's presence is a special privilege. After all, why should we, a people who willingly rebel against God, expect to stand in His presence and be justified? The short, not-so theological answer is we shouldn't. Yet God offers that to us because of His great love. In Matthew 27 we read about the moment Jesus died and how the veil in the Temple tore in half. This veil led to the holy of holies, a place where the Ark of the Covenant was kept and where God's presence was during the Old Testament times. The veil tore when Jesus died because access to God was now direct for anyone and they didn't need a priest because Jesus did the job of bridging the gap. Did you notice the detail of it tearing from top to bottom? That's symbolic, showing God opening the pathway to people, not people opening it to God.

Here's the main connection between Isaiah and Matthew: God imparts His holiness to us so we can be with Him. As we see with Isaiah, God had plans for Him. The same is true for you and me. God has great and glorious plans if we will only decide to be in His presence and take part in His holiness. Yeah, we've messed up and we will again. Isaiah wasn't perfect from that point on. What he was though is called by God and empowered by God because God gave an invitation that Isaiah accepted. I think if we were in that place Isaiah was, we would have done the exact same thing as Isaiah did and realize how utterly broken we are. I think that's what make's God's offer so special. God knew Isaiah was broken and took care of the problem. As the angel Gabriel said to Mary in the book of Luke, "Nothing is impossible with God."

Something to Think About

Imagine yourself in Isaiah's place. What would you do? Would you be different than Isaiah?

How has God made you pure and clean? How is He renewing you?

Consider how God has made you. What could He be calling you to? How does your being made holy relate?

So what? How does your story demonstrate a God of love and mercy? How does that story help others find their way to God?

Day Twenty

Justly Merciful

Read: John 8:1-11

I think this is one of my favorite stories in the Bible. At the very least it has become one of my favorite stories in the Bible. For the adults reading this, you may remember a nod to this story in Mel Gibson's "The Passion of the Christ." For me, that scene cemented this as one of my favorite stories.

In the movie, Jesus has just finished his flogging. It is a grotesque scene that brings life to some of humanities most depraved impulses. The soldiers drag his broken and bloodied body away. Mary, Jesus' mother, kneels down to wipe up her son's blood on the pavement. Another woman kneels with her and helps. As this second woman is doing so, she flashes back to a memory. In the flashback we see in the distance men standing around and in the foreground, we see just the feet of Jesus. Then we see the camera angle shift and it is the perspective of above Jesus. Jesus knelt and began to write in the sand. The camera shot goes back to the foot perspective and we see the men in the background dropping stones and walking away. Just as the last of the men leave, a bloody, dirty, delicate hand reaches towards Jesus' feet. Soon we see a face, just as bloody, dirty, and delicate. She looks up at Jesus. We then get to see Jesus' face. It is not snubbing her or condescending. In fact, it is filled with mercy. He looks down on her and extends His hand to her.

This scene fleshed out perfectly what I imagined the story in the text to look like. We don't know what Jesus wrote, though some speculate. It's not really relevant to the story. What is relevant is how He interacts with her and about her. No, He doesn't say what she was doing is ok. No, He doesn't even demand they find her partner in adultery. Last I checked, adultery is a team sport. He sees the situation for what it is: a woman who was caught doing something wrong but manipulated for the justification of the Pharisees and scribes. The Pharisees and scribes were exactly right regarding what they said in verses four and five. What Jesus rightfully read into the context was the reason why they were wrong.

If you're like my wife, you have a strong sense of justice. That sense of justice can be triggered when someone makes a bad decision on the road or during a bad call at a ball game. This sense goes more than what normal people might want. It demands justice immediately and fully. Depending on the severity of the infraction, I want that too. I know what we sometimes miss is that in our quest for justice, we are missing the bigger context and why we want justice. Though we both believe justice is a part of what we are called to deliver as Christians since God is just, we get caught up in our own personal feelings of it. Sometimes, it's more about us than it is about true justice. It has to do with a feeling of vindication instead of what is right. After all, how many times has God or other people given me a pass on justice in the name of mercy? How many times did God or other people see something bigger at hand then immediate retribution? We don't know who this woman was, but I can almost guarantee she left that situation a new person.

Something to Think About

Think about a time you wanted justice. What was the situation? What would justice have looked like? Did you get it?

Now think about a time you should have received justice but instead got mercy. What did that mean to you? Why do you think you received mercy instead?

Now consider your faith walk. Where do you see God's justice coming in to form you into a better person? How about when you see His mercy doing the same thing?

So what? How do we take this idea of mercy and use it to show others who Jesus is? How can acts of mercy be used to transform normally hard hearts?

Day Twenty-One
A Long Time Coming

Read: Daniel 7:13-14, Luke 22:66-71

Biblical prophecies can be kind of trippy! There are these grand visions and vague descriptions of what the author saw. Then every person with an overactive imagination knows exactly what they were seeing simply based on the vague description. Ever hear these doomsday prophets who know exactly when Jesus is coming back even though no one else does? I guess they have a special connection to God, like a red phone He will call them up on. You can probably guess that these prophets were wrong, on account that you and I are still here and you're reading this thought-provoking devotional. You'd think it's hard to keep all these prophecies straight. Yet, for the audience who read these prophecies, they made sense. Go figure huh? It's like in the "Lord of the Rings" when there's some prophecy about the return of the king and everyone is puzzled when and who but know what to look for.

In the Daniel passage, he has just seen a vision of four beasts and watching them demolish each other. It is a terrifying vision to behold. Then, after Daniel sees this final, terrible beast, he sees this being he calls the Ancient of Days. It doesn't take a seminary degree to know that this is God. Daniel watches as the final terrible beast is slain by the Ancient of Days despite all the boasting and foul words being spoken by the beast. All the other beasts are also undone by the Ancient of Days. Then, Daniel sees this one like the Son of Man. I wonder if Daniel saw the details of this person or what exactly he saw. That term "Son of Man" was well known to the Jews as the Messiah who would rule.

Really cool! (handwritten margin note)

Now fast forward to the passage in Luke. Jesus is before the Council of elders on trial. When asked if He's the Christ, He specifically uses the title "Son of Man" and uses the exact wordage from Daniel 7. Does that explain a little bit why the Council got so mad? He, in no uncertain terms, called Himself God. Now it so happens He was God so you can guess why He used that terminology.

Why is this important? Jesus knew exactly what He was saying. Numerous times in all four gospels we read Jesus quoting the Old Testament phrases to refer to Himself. It has to do with who Jesus claimed to be and if He really was who He said He was. C.S. Lewis, in his book <u>Mere Christianity</u>, considers the claims Jesus made and said that he was (shorthand here) "a liar, lunatic, or Lord." In much more eloquent words Lewis makes the point that the Lord claim is really the only plausible one we can conclude. The question for us as we consider this story and others like it are who do we say Jesus is.

Something to Think About

What would you think of someone walked around claiming to be God? What would be your reaction?

Consider C.S. Lewis' idea about the liar, lunatic, or Lord. What do you think about it?

Who do you say Jesus is? What evidence do you have for it?

So what? What does your claim of who Jesus is have to do with the way you live your life everyday?

Day Twenty-Two

Faithfulness of Christ

Read: Galatians 2

Ever sat down and read all of Galatians? I have to sheepishly admit that, prior to seminary, I never did. Oh sure, I knew about the Fruit of the Spirit (good luck having me rattle them off though). I knew about the, "I have been crucified with Christ" part of chapter two. Those are hallmark passages. Not bad for bumper stickers too! I can't say I've ever been cut off or gotten an angry look from someone who has a bumper sticker with the Fruit of the Spirit.

Chapter one tells of Paul taking a bit of a hiatus after his conversion. I never knew he did that! We see in chapter one that Paul's demeanor is less pleasant than his other letters. He is upset by what he's seeing with the church in Galatia. This leads into chapter two, where Paul gets in Peter's face about being a bit two faced. Paul didn't do the gentle, gingerly Christian etiquette by pulling Peter quietly aside and saying, "Hey man, I really feel like you're not being authentic about who you are. I think we need some accountability with this." Rather, Paul goes toe-to-toe with Peter in front of everybody! This is probably the point where people start shifting uncomfortably and trying not to make eye contact with either of the men. This all leads us to a point I want to highlight in chapter two.

Verse sixteen can be translated in one of two ways. The first is as most of you probably have in your Bibles. Twice the passage uses the term, "faith in Christ" and what that passage says in its context is true. The other translation is a minor variant, which is still true, but I think is a better hermeneutic (how you like that word huh?) that fits the context of the entire Bible. Oh, in case you didn't know, hermeneutic means how you translate and understand the Bible. In this case, the second, "faith in Christ" is translated, "the faithfulness of Christ." This has to do with the faithfulness of Jesus to His mission. Re-read verse 16 again using both variants. If need be, take a minute to re-read the chapter to get the fuller picture.

What does this difference mean? If both translations work and they look like they mean the same thing, who cares? Put on your imagination cap and picture this scene if you will. You have been struggling with something for some time now. It's a spiritual issue and you need guidance, so you see your pastor. You explain your situation to him and seek his advice. Using the first translation as his theology, his advice would sound like this: you need to pray more, read your Bible more, be part of small groups. Don't get me wrong: these are all good things, great things in fact. They do rely on you and your power though. Now imagine all this, but using the second translation as the theology for the advice. His advice would be something like this: spent time knowing who Jesus is and giving this struggle to Him since He has already overcome it. Initially this sounds like a cop out. What does that mean to "know Jesus and give Him this struggle?" This goes to the idea that it's not by your power, but by His. He has conquered sin and death and the grave. He is the one who will give you strength, not because you did an extensive Bible study or recited the Lord's prayer. It is about being acquainted with Jesus and that full reliance on Him. Yes, Bible study, prayer, and other disciplines will help with knowing Jesus. What this second translation says is that those are tools to understand who Jesus is and connecting with Him. What this second translation looks like is asking Jesus into every situation. It looks like seeking wise counsel from people who know and love Jesus. This second translation sees people studying the Bible to know Jesus more, praying to communicate with Jesus, and in small groups because they are growing with others in their relationship with Jesus. It all comes back to Jesus.

What I've noticed in my time as a Christian and youth pastoring is that people tend to forget the reason why we study the Bible, pray, and do other disciplines. It becomes a means to an end or a way to rub the genie's lamp so to speak. It becomes about what we can get from it. That's why I like the second translation better. It fits with the idea we see in the Bible of God calling people to rely on Him and the fullness of life that comes from fellowship with Him. That's what people originally had in Eden and will ultimately have someday when we are in paradise. In the case of Paul in Galatians, he was making the case of Jesus being the way we are sanctified, not because of the doings of the Law. In the same way, our lives are sanctified not because we went through AWANA or completed the Roman Road Bible study. It's because we have a personal, developing, dependent relationship with Jesus.

Something to Think About

Take some time to read the passage again with the two translations and sit on that for a minute or two. How do you see these two translations impacting the story in Galations?

Are your spiritual disciplines deepening your relationship with Jesus or are they checking off the box? What makes you say that?

What would it look like to have a relationship with Jesus that was contingent on the faithfulness of Jesus to His mission?

So what? How does this change in perspective market the Christian lifestyle to people outside the church?

Day Twenty-Three:

My Personal Friend Jesus

Read: John 1:1-18

He's my buddy!

One of the important parts to remember when we read the Bible is that it wasn't written in a void without any kind of context or history to it. Now, that sounds kind of like a, "well duh" statement. You might even be thinking if I'm giving you those kind of ideas as profound, I probably *Amen!* paid too much for my education. Point one: yes, I paid too much. Point two: it's not a profound statement yet it is a mistake that is often made at some point when reading the Bible.

The idea of the Bible being written at a particular time in history to a particular people makes passages like this all the more powerful. Consider other mythologies you may be familiar with from the ancient world. Personally I love the Greek mythology so I think of that when I read passages like this one. The Greek gods were mean and selfish! The whole story of <u>The Illiad</u> (come on you have to have read that by now!) is about how the goddesses messed with some poor prince and *Eww...* pushed him to steal another king's wife, therefore sparking a huge war and destroying a city. Then there's Zeus and his hobby of siring many children. When the gods got involved with people, it didn't go well. When you consider stories like these and other stories from ancient mythologies, the gods seldom act unselfishly on behalf of humanity.

Now bring in the passage we read from John 1. It point blank calls Jesus God right in the first verse. How do we know John's talking about Jesus? The passage describes another John who was a forerunner for Jesus. It says that John was not this God, but came to testify about God. John the Baptist asserts Jesus is God by saying how Jesus has always existed. What was the point for Jesus coming to earth? Right in verse twelve and thirteen it says those who believed in Him became children of God. This isn't like Papa Zeus either. This means inheritance to paradise. This means the fullness of purpose and the fullness of self that comes from knowing the One who created you. Jesus came so people could personally relate to God. Remember all those laws in Leviticus? Those laws about purity and righteousness were set up so people could have God among them in the temple. God, since that fateful day in Eden, has been trying to reestablish relationships with His people.

In the coming days we are going to explore the most pivotal points in human history: the death and resurrection of Jesus. I would be doing you a great disservice in your spiritual walk if I didn't process these events with you. Those are relevant and important because of this passage we read today. God came to earth and lived with people with the sole purpose of buying them back once and for all. No other religions spoke of gods who did that. No religions today speak of that either. It was more than giving people a gift of the sun or animals. It was giving them the right to be heirs to all God has to give. It means being called a son or daughter and all that status gives to them. That, my dear Watson, is profound.

Something to Think About

Think about your favorite myths or stories about ancient gods. What are some stories that described the gods being giving of themselves for the sake of their creation?

What does it mean that the God of all creation was so concerned with His people that He lived life among them?

How does this idea of a God so intimately concerned about you matter on a day to day basis?

So what? What does the fact of a God so in love with His people look like to those people outside of the church? How does the way we internalize that help them know Jesus?

Day Twenty-Four

The Chosen One

Read: Isaiah 53

When I was growing up, I remember counselors in school telling us how we were going to change the world. I remember motivational speakers talking about how our generation would be the ones to change things for the better. I thought I was special. I thought, "Wow! I have this special destiny!" Then I remember hearing these same people say this to the next generation. How could they? Didn't they see the bozos that generation had? I was part of the chosen generation! As I look back, I see the guidance counselors and motivational speakers were trying to sell a destiny to us. It's not a bad destiny. They spoke of aspirations that involved nobility and going farther than the generations before us. The thought was that speaking of this grand destiny to people over and over would hopefully mature into a realization of that destiny.

Destiny is not unique to modern thinking. Did you know the giving of names in the Bible were tied to who the people were? Sometimes the names were ones of noble character such as Ruth (friendship) or Joshua (Yahweh is salvation). They lived up to those names. Then there were names like Chilion (waster) and Mahlon (sickness). If you ever thought yikes... your parents didn't think much of you, you can take comfort that didn't name you sick and wasting. Sadly they also lived up to their names too. Names and destinies were intertwined so much that God changed the names of Abram and Sarai because He had a plan with them that involved bigger destinies, so they needed names that conveyed those destinies.

Enter Jesus into the picture. His name is a derivative of Joshua so check that destiny. He also comes onto the scene after the words of Isaiah 53 were written. He knew this passage was about Him. This was His destiny. Exactly how does one grow up knowing their life will culminate in great suffering? How exactly does that idea that "Yahweh is salvation" come from this immense suffering? Well now that's the great twist of the story. The end of the chapter tells that because of that suffering, He will be exalted and will be the means of God's salvation. How you like that twist M. Night Shyamalan?

Jesus knew this was His destiny from the beginning. He was well acquainted with Genesis 3 and the prophecy of the serpent and the woman's seed. He knew the promise of Abraham to be a blessing to the world. He knew the promise to David that an heir of his will sit on the throne forever. Jesus told His followers over and over that His coronation would be through His suffering. That's because His kingdom was greater than any kingdom they would find on this earth. Yes, His path is one of suffering. Yes, it would be a difficult path to walk. Yes, the destiny He had was worth it. It was worth having His people by His side. It was worth finding a resolution for humanity from day one back in Eden. By walking through these trials and taking the eternal kingship, it gave purpose to people. Their destinies mattered because it fit into the narrative of God using His people for great things. It gives people throughout history the chance to be part of God's love story. Destinies are not often found with ease. That is what makes them so treasured.

Something to Think About

What do you believe is your destiny? If you're not sure, what is your dream destiny?

How does that destiny fit into God's story for humanity?

How has God personally equipped you for that destiny? Who has He put in your life to achieve that?

So what? Why do you think God is so interested in you and your purpose in life? Why does the life, death, and resurrection of Jesus make your story one of hope for others?

Day Twenty-Five

Original Sin

Read: Genesis 3

Got
'Em!

I don't know about you, but I struggle to trust when someone says they will do something. I start out believing they will do what they say, but in the back of my mind I'm ready for the disappointment. This is a way to help cushion the blow when or if they don't come through. If any of you are like that raise your hand (if you just raised your hand while reading this, that is pretty comical). I can tell you where that feeling comes from too. It comes from wanting something and trusting someone for it and in the end being let down. After a time or two of what I thought were big deals I began to distrust as a general rule. Now take that expectation into adulthood and into relationships like marriage and being a parent. Pretty fun stuff I can assure you...

Somewhere along the lines, my hurt little heart began to believe that I would never be taken care of unless I took care of it myself. Professionally this can be good because I make sure a task is done. It can be problematic because I don't delegate and that is something I am always working to improve on. In the end, the issue is trust. That is a central issue in this passage. The serpent twisted the words God spoke by subtly misquoting Him. It really gives credence to the phrase, "the devil is in the details." The serpent twists the words and makes the woman and man second guess whether God will really do what He said. After all, they can just take care of themselves. Never mind they are experiencing paradise where everything they need is provided in one way or another. They can have the ability to care for themselves and not be reliant on someone else. They soon realize what cost comes with being god of your own life.

As they try to remedy the situation, Adam and Eve try to do things on their own. They hide. They make leaf coverings. They rationalize. The idea of going to God and getting help isn't an option on the table. As they find out later, that going to God really is the only option they have. God doesn't undo what they've done. Apologist Frank Turek of Cross Examined is known for stating that God, being loving, gives people the choice to follow Him because love isn't forced. Part of that comes with accepting the consequences that comes. What God does is provide a solution. God doesn't wait for an apology or admission of guilt. Right away He has a plan. That's what is meant in verses fourteen and fifteen. And exactly how do people leverage God's provision? They trust. Proverbs 3:5 sums it up exactly:

> *"Trust in the Lord your God with all your heart*
> *and lean not on your own understanding."*

As I consider my own life, mistrust causes relational rifts in my life. The number of times it actually prevents me from getting hurt are very few. It disrupts the fullness of life I could have with my wife and my kids. It hurts how I relate to my close friends. It makes me suspicious of employers and coworkers. I have to fight the distrust of student's words or the distrust of motives of a parent's question or comment. The same is true with my relationship with Jesus. I am prone to question whether He is who He claimed, if what He came to do was the real deal. In the end, I have a choice to explore my mistrust and validate/debunk it or to play it safe and trust in what I perceive and "know." What I have found is that when I muscle through my distrust and make myself prove my theory or theories, I am pleasantly surprised at who Jesus is revealing Himself to be. As I apply this to my relationships with people, I find myself being pleasantly surprised too. In the end, God is the one I can always rely on, even if I don't agree. I can do this because I see that Jesus was exactly who He said He was and God used Jesus to fulfill that promise He made in Genesis 3. That's where we will be going in the coming days.

Something to Think About

What was a time your trust was broken? How does that affect the way you relate to others? How about the way you relate to God?

Consider how God right away provided a solution for his people even though they didn't trust Him. How does God reach out to you to bridge that gap?

How is God healing your heart so you can impact others for His kingdom?

So what? How does your story of God redeeming you give others hope that Jesus is who He said He is?

Day Twenty-Six

The Reckoning

Read: John 19:1-30

"I remember that day well. I remember exactly where I was that day and what was happening." This saying is said by everyone who lived during a pivotal time in history. My mom could tell you exactly where she was on November 22, 1963 when President Kennedy was assassinated. I can tell you exactly where I was and what was happening on September 11, 2001. Days like those are etched into a person's memory. Days like that are so poignant because of the impact they had on a people. The same goes for good memories too. Just ask any Chicago Cubs fan where they were when the Cubs finally won a World Series.

John 19 comes in the middle of the trial and execution of Jesus. The chapter starts with the flogging of Jesus and the crown of thorns. It then moves to Pilate trying to release Jesus but ultimately giving into the mob. We see the march to the execution site, the nailing process, the hanging on the cross and ultimately the death of Jesus. For those witnessing this event it was a pivotal moment. It was heartbreaking to some to see the One they hoped was the Messiah being put to death. William Lane Craig, in videos proving the Resurrection actually happened, points out the Jews had no concept of a Messiah who would be killed by their enemies and die criminal's death, which in Jewish custom meant he was under the curse of God. To some it was vindication of their piety and devotion to the ways of Moses. It confirmed their way of life would continue. For some it was another spectacle of Roman brutality and enforcement of their will.

This is one of the definitive moments in human history. It is overshadowed by another one that is yet to come. This moment, when the God who was made flesh, the promised one from Genesis 3, is subject to the prophecy of Isaiah 53. Though any good Jew knew the Genesis and Isaiah passages, they may not have recognized it being lived out. The God of the universe took on human flesh and died horribly, knowing that people, by in large, would reject Him. That's what He said in Matthew 7:13-14 when He described the narrow and wide gates. This day would be with the spectators for the rest of their lives and impact the way they lived. Well, that is, this day along with what would happen three days later.

Consider your spiritual journey. The story of Jesus' crucifixion is known to Christian and non-Christian alike. It is etched into the walls of the Sistine Chapel. Johnny Cash and Trent Reznor of Nine Inch Nails used the term, "crown of thorns" in the song "Hurt." Everyone knows the story but few have been impacted by it like those who follow Jesus. What was it like when you first heard the entire story of the crucifixion? Were you a child in Sunday school? Were you an adult who stumbled across it? Were you fighting against God and this story was told to you in a new, fresh way? For some of you reading this you may not follow Jesus. That certainly is your prerogative, but I must ask what this story means to you. If you were to ask anyone who is a true, dedicated follower of Jesus, their assessment of the story is a life changing assessment. If you are reading this and you are a follower of Jesus, consider how that moment of realizing the extent of Jesus' sacrifice changed your life. Consider the long ranging impact it has on who you are and what you do with your life.

Regardless of whether you follow Jesus or not, the death of Jesus is not just a normal execution. It is a death that changed the scope of history in one way or another. This death had to happen, just as it was foretold in Genesis 3. It had to happen because of our evilness. Do you remember when you realized how lost you were? Do you remember when you realized how stuck you were in mess ups and sin? That's why this event had to happen. It gave us a fighting chance to be something better. It gave us that chance to be sons and daughters of God and heirs to what He has. This death had to happen because it opens the door to the biggest event in human history, the event that affirmed Jesus is the Son of God.

Something to Think About

Where were you when you first heard about Jesus' death? What was happening at that time?

Where were you when you realized this death was God's way to buy you back from hell? If you aren't there yet, what does all this mean to you?

What do you imagine is the cost of Jesus leaving heaven, only to be killed by people who are mostly going to reject Him? What impact does that have on the sacrifice and the love God has for His people?

So what? What does your story about God's sacrifice mean to the way you live your life daily? How does your story impact those around you who don't know the full story of Jesus?

Day Twenty-Seven
The Crowning of the King

Read: John 20

Ever have one of moments that was a, "this changed everything" moment? It completely changes the way you see something. One example is when I was fourteen and got a job in a restaurant. I was a bus boy, so nothing too lofty. That moment of change for me was seeing how the food is made in a restaurant. Now, I never thought it was a super special process or that elves worked in the back doing the work. You see, my mom says I'm smart so I know things like it's not elves making my food. Working in a restaurant does take a little bit of the mystery away from the process or takes away from the magic of it all. I saw foods sometimes get microwaved or certain foods prepackaged. I also saw new ways to do things. After working in a restaurant, for example, I now bake my bacon. I'm bakin' my bacon (I know, bad joke). It really works! I save myself the splatters from grease and the burns that come from it and it tastes oh so good! I'm talking melt in your mouth good!

Yesterday I mentioned the pivotal moment in human history. That moment is found in every gospel account. I focused on John for a reason that we'll cover in a bit. After dying and being buried, the story come to an empty tomb of Jesus. The empty tomb changed everything! Just exactly how? It validates everything the Bible had covered in the Old Testament. It gave direction and purpose to the New Testament. Apologist William Lane Craig had a conversation with Ben Shapiro in May of 2019 and during that time they talked religion. Dr. Craig is a Christian and Ben is a practicing Orthodox Jew, so the issue of the resurrection came up. Dr. Craig said that the God raising Jesus from the dead was God's confirmation of who Jesus claimed to be.

The question of who Jesus is determines whether we take Him seriously or not. C.S. Lewis didn't seem to think there was any question of who Jesus was based on the evidence. He said that Jesus was either a liar, a lunatic, or Lord. Videos on Dr. Craigs website www.reasonablefaith.org give evidence to the resurrection and ask what we make of the evidence. When we consider the empty tomb, the appearances of a resurrected Jesus, and the changed lives of the disciples, we are forced to rationalize what we make of those facts and what this means about who Jesus is. As much as some have tried to find naturalistic reasons for those three facts, the reasons just don't work. The most compelling and plausible explanation is that God raised Jesus from the dead. After all, if God created the heavens and the earth, what's a resurrection to Him?

The resurrection is a "this changed everything" moment. It really doesn't matter if people believe it or not. Jesus was foretold from Genesis and the by prophets. A picture of Him was given in Isaiah 53. He fulfilled those duties by suffering torture and death on a cross. The resurrection is the coronation to His Kingship. This resurrection means that when He said He was the Son of Man, He wasn't making this up to trigger people. It means when He said all authority has been given unto Him, He really did have it. It means when He says He can give eternal life, He really can. The reason I chose this passage over the other gospel accounts is because of what is said in 20:30-31. All these things, the life of Jesus, were written so we can believe and have eternal life. There is plenty of evidence to be found confirming what John and the other gospel writers wrote is true. If what they say is true, that means Jesus is the Son of God and salvation comes through Him. That is the gospel message. That message changes everything.

Something to Think About

Consider the three facts of the resurrection: the empty tomb, the appearances of a resurrected Jesus, and the changed lives of the disciples. How do you account for these three facts? What is your rationale?

Do you think Jesus was a liar, a lunatic, or Lord? Why?

Read the other resurrection accounts in the gospels. What do they claim about Jesus? Why is this important?

So what? Who do you say Jesus is? How has that impacted your lives on a daily basis? Why is this important for others to know about?

Day Twenty-Eight

Deep Dish Discoveries

Read: Acts 2

OmG!

There was a day in my life that changed me forever. I have to give credit to my youth pastor for it too. I was on a mission trip in Chicago. Part of what we were doing there was to experience cultures different than our own and ones that were part of the Chicago culture. Part of that was trying different foods. Then the day came that we tried Chicago style pizza. Oh what a marvelous day! The deep, rich crust with loads of toppings. It takes a while to bake but oh so worth it! From that day on it has been my favorite style of pizza. I may hate their baseball and football teams, but I certainly love their pizza.

Ok, so this is a stupid example of being changed by something, but I think it illustrates how people are changed by events on a small scale. Now if you're a purveyor of fine foods like me, eating something so delightful is a big deal. Even so, it doesn't compare to what we see in Acts 2. This is roughly a month and a half after Jesus rose from the dead to when He ascended. He has made numerous appearances to His disciples and others (see 1 Corinthians 15 for a list of people who saw the resurrected Jesus). I'm not exactly sure how much time has elapsed since the ascension. Regardless, the disciples are waiting in Jerusalem just as Jesus instructed them. Then the Holy Spirit comes and nothing is the same.

If you breeze over the first thirteen verses, you can see this marked change by the disciples and it's understandable why they are mistaken for being drunk. This is unlike anything they have ever done! To further that point, only about two months ago were these men hiding and cowering from the authorities. When Jesus was arrested, they all fled and were in hiding after Jesus was executed. They were afraid of the authorities stringing them up too. That's why Peter denied Jesus. Now we see those men, with Peter leading the way, proudly and boldly proclaiming the risen Jesus. How could they be the same men? Dr. William Lane Craig, J. Warner Wallace, and Lee Strobel all point to this radical change in the disciple's actions as proof of the risen Jesus, among other points of proof. What could cause these meek, mostly blue collared, mostly uneducated men to proclaim something so boldly that most would die for it? The answer: they experienced the resurrected Jesus. The same Jesus they spent three and a half years in close community with was killed before their very eyes. Everything He said was now left hanging. When they saw the resurrected Jesus and saw Him eat, drink, and felt His piercings, all that Jesus said was fulfilled. He was the Son of Man that Daniel foretold. Paul says it best in Romans 8:31

> *"What then shall we say to these things?*
> *If God is for us, who can be against us?"*

Again, my story of experiencing one of the greatest culinary creations known to man pales in comparison to the transforming experience of the resurrected Jesus. It is but a simple comparison. Ponder this to yourselves as you take some reflection time: what was a transformative experience in your life? Now look at how Jesus transformed your life. If you are reading this and you claim Jesus as Lord, you can look back at your life and see how Jesus is adjusting you and molding you. The Holy Spirit whispers to you the way to go and encourages a lifestyle aligned with God. It's not a final process by any means but rather a continuous transformative process. If you are reading this and you are not a follower of Jesus or curious about it, may I encourage you to talk to others who are committed followers of Jesus. I want to emphasize the committed part so you get an accurate picture of following Jesus and not from someone who follows Jesus just on Sunday or during small group. This transformation is, in my assessment, one of the biggest cases for the cause of Christ. This is how people can discover who God is and what He is doing for people.

Something to Think About

Consider a transformative experience in your life. What was it like? What happened? How did it change you?

Consider when you first asked Jesus into your heart and what happened afterwards. How were you in the process of becoming different? What differences can you see from before Jesus and after Jesus?

Who do you say Jesus is? What about your life proclaims that?

How does your testimony make that claim? How does the change in you demonstrate what God has done and is doing in your life to others?

Day Twenty-Nine

Hold the Line

Read: Ephesians 6:10-20

Here's a fun fact about me: I have my black belt in the martial arts. I started when I was about 8 and got my black belt when I was 14. A big part of being in the martial arts was about avoiding a fight. Sounds kind of ironic since the whole idea of martial arts is, you know, the martial part. The idea was that having to fight is a last resort. We are taught to find other ways to solve our problems. As I'm sure anyone who went through high school knows, there are some times when people aren't really interested in talking. In those cases, be it rare, that's when the martial arts can prove useful. Thankfully I never had to use it and I hope that remains the case.

When we read this passage in Ephesians, it's easy to picture a Roman solider all dressed up in armor looking fierce. The truth is: that's not really the language Paul is using in this case. Imagine talking to people who are part of the Roman empire and comparing a religion to being like a Roman soldier. These Romans conquered people and treated others terribly. It would've scared many of them away! Instead, Paul uses the imagery of a gladiator. This gives the picture of a warrior who is not armored all the way up and well suited for combat, but instead someone who is fighting defensive and holding the line. It gives a whole different picture to what we visualize.

What does this have to do with our spiritual walk? The whole book of Ephesians is Paul making the case that the way of Jesus is superior to the way they did things before. Ephesians used to be involved in black magic so when Paul comes and introduces Jesus, it is a radically different way of communing with the spiritual realm. Verse ten says it best: be strong in the Lord and in the strength of His might. You see, Jesus already won the fight. His death and resurrection were a coronation to His kingship. He has conquered and reigns victorious. We aren't asked to go on a conquest in the name of the Lord. We are asked to hold tight against the darkness in this realm. The truth is that we aren't strong enough to go on a conquest. Since subjugation with force isn't really God's M.O., He's not behind us on a conquest. He sent Jesus on a different conquest mission and Jesus did it. We are called to fight for what is true and good in this world and be His ambassadors. Just like when I was in the martial arts, it wasn't about picking fights and being the biggest brawler around. It was about defending.

Now let me be clear: it's not saying we can't start conversations and debates. That's not what the passage is saying. The passage is saying that our battle is about the unseen such as ideas, values, beliefs, and even the spiritual beings. It's also saying our job is to be ready to engage these aspects of life. I would argue this gives reason to understand apologetics. That means being able to rationalize your beliefs and know how to defend them. Our faith is not a passive one, yet we don't have to fret about getting it all right because Jesus has fought for us. Personally, I'm glad I don't need to make it perfect and get a spiritual head count. What I need to do is be able to tell others about what I believe and why. I can handle that.

Something to Think About

How many people do you know that are "strong armed" into believing? Do you think you'd believe in someone's ideas because they forced you to?

How can you rely on Jesus' strength for everyday battles? How does His victory help you everyday?

Run through the armor of God. What parts of life do you see these divinely empowered pieces of armor affecting?

So what? How do your spiritual battles tell others about the God you serve and the God who has overcome it all?

Day Thirty

Faithfully Thinking

Read: John 20:30-31, 1 Peter 3:13-16

There are some things in this world that are great on their own, but if you combine them together, it is just horrible. An example is orange juice after brushing your teeth. Have you done this? Orange juice is *So good.* Toothpaste, though not appetizing, it still fine on its own. Now if *Gross!* you bring them together, it is just disgusting! I had a friend who told me about a trip she took to Wisconsin Dells and she had chocolate covered cheese curds. Yes, in Wisconsin we will go to that level! Chocolate is great! Cheese curds are great! Together, according to my friend, it was one of the grossest things she had ever eaten. I could go on and I'm sure you could too. I think faith and reason are thought of like this too. Faith is great! Reason is great! Putting them together though, it seems like a contradiction.

I argue that they are not opposites but rather complimentary. How can you trust me? Well, I did write a book so that must mean I'm trustworthy (then again so did the guy who started Scientology...). I did a study with students in 2018 through the book <u>Cold Case Christianity.</u> The book is written by former cold case detective J. Warner Wallace. He was an atheist and decided one day to use his cold case training to test the gospels, specifically the resurrection. He was prompted to do this because of how people would answer when asked, "Why do you believe what you believe?" He found Christians gave similar answers to his Morman family members. So off he started on his intellectual journey. It is like how Lee Strobel used his investigative skills to research the gospels. Just like Strobel, Wallace came to conclude the resurrection was true and became a follower of Jesus. That led him into further study of the Bible and he spent time as a youth pastor and now a public speaker helping people be able to rationalize their faith. When asked about how faith and reason can possibly work together, he noted how the evidence he found brought him to the point where he could make a leap of faith.

I have to full heartedly agree with J. Warner Wallace. I think its easy to dismiss something like logic and reason in Christianity because of passages like Ephesians 2:8-9 where it says we are saved by faith, not works. I get it, really I do. I then would have to ask, "If something is true, is it of God?" The book of John has us questioning what is truth. This is the question Pilate asks Jesus in His interrogation. This comes not long after Jesus says in 14:6 that He is the way, the truth, and the life. While talking to the woman at the well in John 4, Jesus says God is spirit and we have to worship Him in spirit and in truth. As we can see, truth is an important part of God's character. In fact, it seems to be a part of who He is. It can be concluded that if God is the source of truth because He is truth, then all truth is God's truth.

Here's the point: reason and logic direct us to what is true. They argue for truth and give validation. Just as was the case with Strobel, Wallace, and countless others, the facts led them to make steps of faith because they could trust what they discovered. Jesus performed signs to give people reason to believe Him. In the Old Testament, God used signs and wonders to prove Himself too. Remember the story of Moses and the Exodus? God used the plagues as a sign of judgment and a sign of who He was. It's part of the reason the Jews have all those festivals: to remember who God is because of the evidence He has given them. Faith and reason really aren't that opposing. Reason can bring people to faith and faith can prompt people to rationalize what they believe and why. If you look through the references for this entire devotional, you'll see some great resources to help you better understand what you believe and why. These resources can also help you feel confident in taking steps of faith. It will all help to make you a well rounded person and you won't get a disgusting taste in your mouth like you would with orange juice and toothpaste.

Something to Think About

Why do you believe what you believe? How often have you thought about it?

Think of something you're passionate about like a hobby or food. What reasons do you give to rationalize your passion for that? How are you able to rationalize your faith?

Have you met people who have arguments for why they don't believe in Christianity? How can faith and reason help you make connections with them and share the gospel?

So what? How can you grow in your relationship with Jesus by using your head and heart? How does this share that message with a dying world?

Epilogue

Oh. My. Goodness. You did it. Thirty days and you made it. Oh and if you read this in February and you're OCD, then my apologies. I bet you feel holier now. I bet you feel the holiness flowing off you like warmth from a space heater. The other people at church are going to notice. The "I'm blessed" people will rise up and call you blessed. The people who do the 100 meter dash out the door after the last song will stick around to bask in your presence. I'm thinking sonnets will be composed in your honor.

Ok, so maybe I'm exaggerating. Maybe slightly. I do want to commend you for sticking to this for thirty days. My hope is that you have grown in your faith through it. My prayer is that you have new understandings and new ideas because of these last thirty days. Christianity isn't a religion where you get the, "Get out of Eternal Punishment Free Card" and take a seat to wait until Jesus comes back. It is a relationship with God and like any other relationship with someone it takes work and learning more about the person you're in a relationship with and learning about yourself. I hope this devotional has pushed you forward in that sense.

Now, as a way to commemorate your hard work, there is a certificate in the following pages. You can hang it on your fridge and impress all your friends and family. On a side note, an added perk is now if someone is jealous of that certificate, they have to buy my book because you used the only one in the book. This is my path to being a millionaire.

Thank you for being a part of this journey. May you be blessed because of the journey. May you fall more in love with Jesus and His creation because of this time spent contemplating your faith and taking steps to put it into action. If I don't see you soon, I'll see you in paradise.

Mike Neumann

Author Supreme

Certificate of Achievement

This certificate is presented to

In recognition of completing *A Serious Devotional For the Not So Serious*

Signature

Date

About the Author

Mike Neumann has been a youth pastor since 2006. He's a huge fan of the teenage phase of life, and loves to hang out with teens doing crazy stuff while having deep talks. He lives with his wife and three kids in the suburbs of the twin cities, and in his free time, enjoys Xbox, kayaking, and philosophical conversations with his inflatable duck.

References Boring ☺ legal stuff

Day Two

Overview, Luke Ch. 1-9. The Bible Project. The Bible Project, 2016. https://www.youtube.com/watch?v=XIb_dCIxzr0&list=PLH0Szn1yYNecanpQqdixWAm3zHdhY2kPR&index=7.

Day Three

Fear, Credibility, and the Threat of a Police State . Prager University, 2020. https://www.prageru.com/video/ep-133-fear-credibility-and-the-threat-of-a-police-state/.

Day Nine

Prager, Dennis. "The Key to Unhappiness." PragerU. PragerU, November 20, 2017. https://www.prageru.com/video/the-key-to-unhappiness/.

Day Eleven

21 Years. (2020, January 9). *Broadcast Music Inc.* Retrieved August 3, 2020, from https://www.youtube.com/watch?v=eSV-pRGbg4k

Day Thirteen

Mackie, T., & Collins, J. (Directors). (2018, November 1). *The Way of The Exile* [Video file]. Retrieved August 3, 2020, from https://bibleproject.com/explore/way-of-the-exile/

Day Nineteen

Mackie, Tim, and Jon Collins. "The Holiness of God: BibleProject™," March 17, 2015. https://bibleproject.com/explore/holiness/.

Day Twenty

The Passion of the Christ. Film. Icon Productions, 2004.

Day Twenty-One

Lewis, C. S. *Mere Christianity*. New York, NY: Harpercollins Publishers, 2017.

Day Twenty-Five

Turek, Dr. Frank. God's Love and the Problem of Hell, 2018. https://www.youtube.com/watch?v=9gEbkZvn3S4.

Day Twenty-Six

Craig, Dr. William Lane. Did Jesus Rise From the Dead, 2019. https://www.youtube.com/watch?v=4qhQRMhUK1o.

Johnny Cash. *Hurt*. CD. Rick Rubin, 2002.

Nine Inch Nails. *Hurt*. CD. Los Angeles, CA: Trent Reznor, 1994.

Day Twenty-Seven

Craig, Dr. William Lane. Did Jesus Rise From the Dead, 2019. https://www.youtube.com/watch?v=4qhQRMhUK1o.

Lewis, C. S. *Mere Christianity*. New York, NY: Harpercollins Publishers, 2017.

Day Twenty-Eight

Craig, Dr. William Lane. Did Jesus Rise From the Dead, 2019. https://www.youtube.com/watch?v=4qhQRMhUK1o.

Strobel, Lee. *The Case for Easter: Investigating the Evidence for the Resurrection*. Grand Rapids, MI: Zondervan, 2018.

Wallace, J. Warner. *Cold-Case Christianity: a Homicide Detective Investigates the Claims of the Gospels*. Colorado Springs, CO: David C Cook, 2013.

Day Thirty

Wallace, J. Warner. *Cold-Case Christianity: a Homicide Detective Investigates the Claims of the Gospels*. Colorado Springs, CO: David C Cook, 2013.

Printed in the United States
by Baker & Taylor Publisher Services